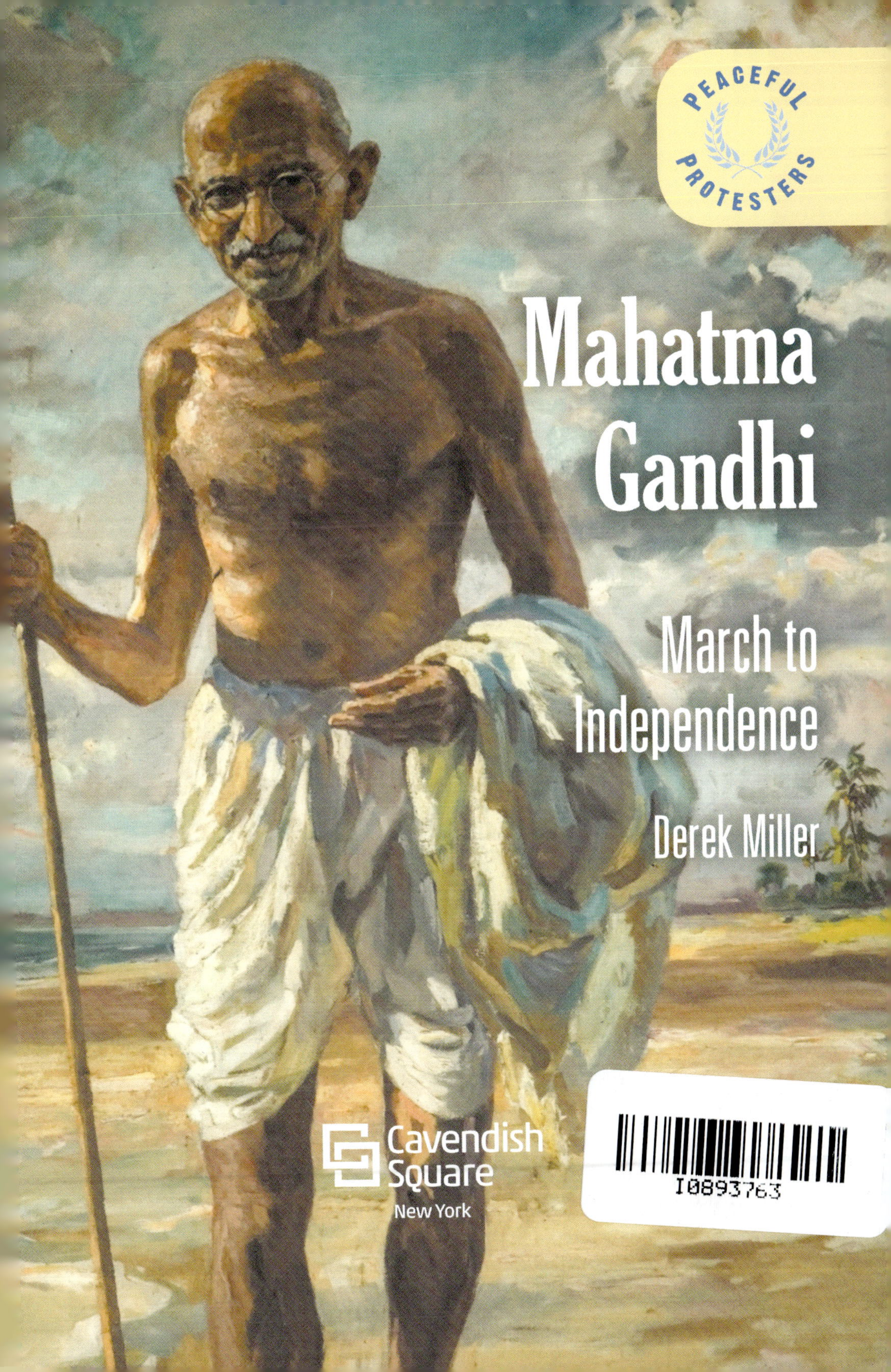

Peaceful Protesters

Mahatma Gandhi

March to Independence

Derek Miller

Cavendish Square
New York

Published in 2018 by Cavendish Square Publishing, LLC
243 5th Avenue, Suite 136, New York, NY 10016

First Edition

Library of Congress Cataloging-in-Publication Data

Names: Miller, Derek L., author.
Title: Mahatma Gandhi : march to independence / Derek Miller.
Description: New York : Cavendish Square Publishing, 2018. | Series: Peaceful protesters | Includes bibliographical references and index.
Identifiers: LCCN 2017022535 (print) | LCCN 2017022929 (ebook) | ISBN 9781502631145 (library bound) | ISBN 9781502633965 (Paperback) | ISBN 9781502631152 (E-book)
Subjects: LCSH: Gandhi, Mahatma, 1869-1948--Juvenile literature. | Statesmen--India--Biography--Juvenile literature. | Nationalists--India--Biography--Juvenile literature. | Lawyers--India--Biography--Juvenile literature. | India--Politics and government--1919-1947--Juvenile literature. | South Africa--Politics and government--1836-1909--Juvenile literature.
Classification: LCC DS481.G3 (ebook) | LCC DS481.G3 M4735 2018 (print) | DDC 954.03/5092 [B] --dc23
LC record available at https://lccn.loc.gov/2017022535

Editorial Director: David McNamara
Editor: Caitlyn Miller
Copy Editor: Nathan Heidelberger
Associate Art Director: Amy Greenan
Designer: Alan Sliwinski
Production Coordinator: Karol Szymczuk
Photo Research: J8 Media

The photographs in this book are used by permission and through the courtesy of: Cover, p 1 Pep Roig/Alamy Stock Photo; p. 3 and throughout; ilolab/Shutterstock.com; p. 4 Pictorial Press Ltd/Alamy Stock Photo; p. 9, 15, 50, 61, 66, 70, 73 Dinodia Photos/Alamy Stock Photo; p. 20 Sanjay Acharya/Wikimedia Commons/File:God Vishnu with Lakshmi and Saraswati.jpg/CC BY-SA 3.0; p. 22 Universal History Archive/Universal Images Group/Getty Images; p. 24 adamkaz/iStockphoto; p. 29 PlaneMad/Wikimedia Commons/File:Indian Revolt of 1857 states map.svg/CC BY-SA 3.0; p. 32 M. Burahnudin/Wikimedia Commons/File:Group portrait of the Maharaja of Mysore and his brothers and sisters.jpg/CC PD; p. 38 Discott/Wikimedia Commons/File:Great Trek map full.png/CC BY-SA 4.0; p. 40 Stapleton Historical Collection/Heritage Image Partnership Ltd/Alamy Stock Photo; p. 42 Hulton Archive/Getty Images; p. 46 Dave Davis, Acme Newspictures Inc./Library of Congress/Wikimedia Commons/File:Gandhi and Nehru 1942.jpg/CC PD; p. 55 Author Unknown/Wikimedia Commons/File:Gandhi Boer War.jpg/CC PD; p. 63 Diego Delso/Wikimedia Commons/File:Jallianwala Bagh-Amritsar-India09.jpg/CC BY-SA 4.0; p. 75 No 9 Army Film & Photographic Unit, Imperial War Museums/Wikimedia Commons/File:Mountbatten Jinnah.jpg/CC PD; p. 76 saiko3p/iStockphoto; p. 79 AP Photo; p. 83 indianarmy.nic.in/Wikimedia Commons/File:Indian soldiers fighting in 1947.jpg/CC PD; p. 84 Margaret Bourke-White/The LIFE Picture Collection/Getty Images; p. 86 AF Archive/Alamy Stock Photo; p. 88 Laurent MAOUS/Gamma-Rapho/Getty Images; p. 91 Dick De Marsico, World Telegram, Library of Congress/ Wikimedia Commons/File:Martin Luther King Jr NYWTS.jpg/CC PD; p. 98 Trevor Samson/AFP/Getty Images.

Printed in the United States of America

CONTENTS

Mahatma Gandhi (1869–1948) was a pioneer of nonviolent resistance.

CHAPTER ONE

Who Was Mahatma Gandhi?

Few people in history have risen to the level of fame of **Mahatma** Gandhi. His name is forever associated with peace and nonviolence, and his deep spiritual beliefs have inspired people internationally. In India, he is still called the Father of the Nation thanks to his role in securing the nation's independence. All around the world, streets bear his name and statues can be found in his likeness. His achievements were staggering, and his importance to India and those he has inspired cannot be overstated.

Yet Gandhi's successes were hard won. Behind the fame and veneration, there was a man who faced numerous struggles in life. His childhood was marked by intense shyness. In fact, he found it difficult to even talk to strangers for many years. This was a challenge he would be forced to overcome to become the noted public speaker of his later years. Likewise, his early law career was disastrous. Having spent much of his family's money on his education, Gandhi proved unable to start a practice or find lucrative employment. His first time in court, he was unable to utter a word when called upon. Gandhi recalls the incident in his autobiography:

> “
>
> *I appeared for the defendant and had thus to cross-examine the* ***plaintiff****'s witnesses. I stood up, but my heart sank into my boots. My head was reeling and I felt as though the whole court was doing likewise. I could think of no question to ask. The judge must have laughed, and the [lawyers] no doubt enjoyed the spectacle. But I was past seeing anything. I sat down and told the agent that I could not conduct the case.*

He fled the courtroom in embarrassment.

Gandhi's story might have fizzled out here if he had given up on his dreams. But he did not. He tried again and again to practice law, despite numerous setbacks. In the end, his attempts landed him in the position to challenge injustice and racism, first in South Africa and later in India. It was in this role that his character truly shone through and he influenced the course of human history.

When he witnessed injustice in South Africa, Gandhi did not shy away from it, nor did he respond with violence. Instead, he answered injustice with truth. He developed the strategy of **Satyagraha**—a **Sanskrit** word that means "truth force." Satyagraha's core message was a call for nonviolent resistance to injustice. Gandhi organized Indians in South Africa to refuse to follow laws that humiliated and persecuted them. While this may appear to be typical passive resistance at first—refusing to follow a law that one disagrees with—Gandhi was careful to distinguish Satyagraha from all forms of passive resistance that came before it.

Previously, passive resistance had been used by movements such as the women's suffrage movement, which sought to secure the right to vote for women. However, Gandhi saw these historical instances of passive resistance as confrontational. Furthermore, they occasionally involved the use of violence, which he saw as unforgivable. On this subject, Gandhi wrote:

> "
>
> *Passive resistance is often looked upon as a preparation for the use of force while Satyagraha can never be side by side with the use of arms.*

Satyagraha and brute force, being each a negation of the other, can never go together. Satyagraha may be offered to one's nearest and dearest; passive resistance can never be offered to them unless of course they have ceased to be dear and become an object of hatred to us.

Gandhi's innovation of Satyagraha was the marriage of passive resistance with **ahimsa**—or nonviolence. Ahimsa is a religious principle found in three major Indian religions: Hinduism, Buddhism, and Jainism. It calls for complete nonviolence or harmlessness. Jain monks follow this ideal so closely that they carry a broom to sweep small insects out of their way before sitting down so as not to crush them. To Gandhi, ahimsa was absolutely essential in life. It was the font of spirituality, and no action was worth doing if it harmed another being.

Through this melding of passive resistance and ahimsa, Gandhi created his original strategy of Satyagraha to combat injustice. It made an incredible impact. He successfully led campaigns in both South Africa and India to bring about social and political change peacefully. His methods inspired future leaders like Martin Luther King Jr. to also use peaceful means to end injustice and cemented Gandhi's reputation as one of the most influential leaders of the twentieth century.

Karamchand Gandhi, the father of Mahatma, was an important politician in his home state.

Early Life

Mohandas Karamchand Gandhi was born in Porbandar, India, on October 2, 1869. His family belonged to the merchant **caste** of Indian society—below the priestly and ruling castes, but above the laborers and **untouchables**. However, the men of Gandhi's family had a long history of being important political figures. Gandhi's father served as the prime minister of the small state of Porbandar as well as several important cities nearby.

Gandhi's early childhood was relatively typical. He was not an exceptional student, nor did he seem marked for greatness as a leader. Later in life, he recalled being so shy that he ran home from school every day so that no one could talk to him in the street. Nevertheless, some of Gandhi's experiences as a child would shape his later years. One day, he saw a play about Harishchandra, a legendary Indian king who always told the truth and kept his promises. The play moved Gandhi. It inspired his deep conviction in the power of the truth, and this belief would be central to his later protests. Gandhi's mother also influenced him. She was a deeply pious woman who fasted regularly and prayed devotedly. Her deep spiritual convictions undoubtedly helped shape Gandhi's own spirituality.

Gandhi entered high school at the age of eleven after passing the entrance exam. At the age of thirteen, he married Kasturba, who was to be his lifelong partner. She was just fourteen when they wed. A marriage at this age was not uncommon at the time, but Gandhi was later critical of his father for arranging it. He counseled parents to forego child marriages when he was an adult.

Bad Company

It was during high school that Gandhi fell in with the wrong crowd. He became close friends with another student, who encouraged him to eat meat. This was forbidden by his religion, and he had never before done so. His family were strict Hindus and never served meat at home. However, Gandhi's friend convinced him that meat would make him stronger, and he showed off his own speed and strength that far exceeded Gandhi's. This reasoning resonated with Gandhi. Gandhi believed that if Indians ate meat they might be able to drive the British from their country. (The British had begun colonizing India centuries earlier, gaining more power and territory as time went on.) In this way, Gandhi convinced himself that it was his patriotic duty to eat meat. He hid this from his parents to avoid upsetting them.

In the company of the same friend, Gandhi also stole coins to buy cigarettes to smoke. He did so in secret. Once again, he hid the truth from his parents. This was a radical departure from the earlier and later stages of his life, when he valued the truth above all else. But like many people, Gandhi made mistakes during high school. The greatest of these mistakes was stealing a bit of gold from his brother. However, Gandhi immediately confessed his crime to his father. He expected to be struck for his actions, but his father wept rather than punish Gandhi. His father's tears touched Gandhi; he also wept and promised never again to steal. Gandhi would never forget this moment of paternal love, and it figured into his later philosophy that love and nonviolence were, in fact, more powerful than violence.

Leaving India

Gandhi graduated from high school in 1887. He then went to college in the nearby city of Bhavnagar, but he did not do well. He struggled in his classes and returned home unhappy at the end of the first term. Luckily, a family friend visited during this time and recommended that he continue his studies in England rather than return to college in India. Studying in England would allow him to become a lawyer much quicker than he could if he remained in India. A degree in law was necessary for him to follow in his father's footsteps to become an important political leader in his home state.

Gandhi was eager to make the journey and avoid going to college in Bhavnagar. However, his family was less certain. While his brother supported the idea, his mother and his uncle—the oldest living male in his extended family after his father died in 1885—were opposed to the idea. They thought it was irreligious to go to England and that it would be easy for Gandhi to lose his way and forget his heritage if he went abroad. They were worried that he would fall into the habits of eating meat and drinking alcohol when he was alone in the foreign land.

In the end, his uncle agreed that Gandhi could depart if he won his mother's blessing. To accomplish this, Gandhi made three sacred vows before a monk. He swore to not touch wine, women, or meat. This assured his mother that he would make the most of his time in England and not fall into vice.

Gandhi set off for Mumbai (then called Bombay). From there, he planned to sail to England, but before he could depart, he was called before the leaders of his caste. They were deeply skeptical of his proposed trip abroad, and they informed him that it was forbidden, on religious grounds, for him to travel to England. In their opinion, it would be impossible for him to remain a devout Hindu member of the merchant caste surrounded by people eating meat and drinking alcohol. However, Gandhi refused to listen to their advice. Always shy and averse to conflict until this point in his life, he appeared before the elders and informed them that he still intended to go to England. They cursed at him and told him that he would now be an outcast and that other members of the caste would be forbidden from helping him on his trip. But Gandhi remained resolute, and he sailed for England soon after. He left his wife and son behind.

The trip to England was a difficult one. Most of the food served on the ship was not vegetarian, and Gandhi was serious about keeping the promises he'd made to secure his mother's blessing. Gandhi's shyness and inexperience speaking English meant he was unwilling to ask what food did not contain meat. Instead, he ate relatively little. He lived on sweets brought with him from India and porridge. Too shy and embarrassed about his diet to mingle with the other passengers, he spent his time alone in his cabin. One English passenger who did go out of his way to befriend Gandhi urged him to eat meat for his own health. He argued it was necessary in the cooler climate of England. While vegetarianism might be possible in India, it was impossible in the North, the man claimed. But Gandhi was unwilling to compromise because of the vow he took to please his mother. While he planned to eat meat on his return to India, he refused to break his sacred vow to forego eating it while on his travels.

Life in England

In England, Gandhi also found life difficult. He quickly overcame his shyness about speaking English and was able to make some English friends and navigate the alien city. But his vegetarianism remained a constant problem. At first, he boarded with English families who were confused by his unusual diet and were unable to provide him with suitable food. They served him porridge, bread, and boiled vegetables, but barely enough for him not to starve. Not wanting to impose on his hosts, Gandhi did not ask for more.

One close English friend he made repeatedly tried to convince Gandhi to eat meat. Fearful for his health, he urged him to abandon his vow so that he would not grow too weak from hunger. Yet Gandhi still refused to consider the idea. He dreamed of returning to India, but he knew that he must first finish his three years of study in London and somehow keep his vow to his mother in the process.

Gandhi dressed as an English gentleman during his early years before later adopting his distinctive traditional Indian attire.

At one point, Gandhi decided that he ought to become a proper English gentleman. He spent money on fine suits and fashionable hats, as well as violin lessons. However, in the end he realized he was not going to spend his life in London, and it would be better for him to live simply and spare his family the expenses of life as a gentleman. He rented a single room with a stove and began to cook his own breakfast, simple porridge, to save money. He ate lunch out in vegetarian restaurants and had bread for dinner. In this way, he managed to drastically reduce his spending, and this marked his first experiment with living simply. From this point on, simple living would recur as a theme throughout his life.

It also was during this time that Gandhi's view toward vegetarianism shifted radically. He read a pamphlet by a prominent English social reformer named Henry Stephens Salt. The pamphlet, *A Plea for Vegetarianism*, convinced Gandhi that vegetarianism was, in fact, the right course of action in life, not just a vow that he had to keep to his mother. In his autobiography, Gandhi describes his newfound enthusiasm for vegetarianism in the following way:

> "
>
> *A convert's enthusiasm for his new religion is greater than that of a person who is born in it. Vegetarianism was then a new cult in England,*

and likewise for me, because, as we have seen, I had gone there a convinced meat-eater, and was intellectually converted to vegetarianism later. Full of the ***neophyte****'s zeal for vegetarianism, I decided to start a vegetarian club in my locality, Bayswater.*

Perhaps most important, Gandhi also took up the study of religious texts during his time in London. It was two Englishmen who introduced Gandhi to the Bhagavad Gita—one of the most important Hindu scriptures. Despite his upbringing, Gandhi had never read it until that time. He also read the Bible and stories about the life of the Buddha. These texts impressed Gandhi greatly. He saw similarities across these three religions of Hinduism, Christianity, and Buddhism—namely, the idea that "renunciation was the highest form of religion." This idea would inform his thinking for the rest of his life.

On June 10, 1891, Gandhi passed the bar and qualified as a lawyer. Just two days later, he set sail for India, anxious to return home. He had learned much about life in the West during his time in London, and he had traveled to other places in Europe, such as Paris. But surprisingly, the most important event was the emergence of his new attitude toward his own heritage and faith. His devotion to vegetarianism and newfound interest in Hindu religious texts would prove essential to his later life.

Home—for a Short Time

Gandhi arrived back in India in the city of Mumbai. There, he tried to set up his own law practice. His family was heavily indebted due to his schooling in London and his brother's spending with the expectation of Gandhi's successful law career. However, business in Mumbai was slow. Gandhi found that although he had passed the bar, he had no real experience practicing law. When he finally secured a case, it did not go as planned. The first time he appeared in court, he was unable to utter a word when the time came for him to cross-examine a witness. He gave his client her money back and dropped the case.

Gandhi moved to Rajkot, a city closer to home, where he hoped to use his brother's connections to earn more money. But this too ended poorly. His brother was in trouble with a local English official—one whom Gandhi had met briefly in London. His brother convinced Gandhi to go intercede on his behalf because of their acquaintance. However, when Gandhi arrived and launched into his defense of his brother, the Englishman was uninterested in listening and ordered him to leave. Gandhi continued speaking and was forcibly led out by a servant. Gandhi threatened to bring a lawsuit before hearing that such abuses by the English were quite common and nothing would come of a lawsuit other than more trouble.

Unable to effectively practice law at home under this English officer who now keenly disliked him, Gandhi's future was in trouble. Luckily, word reached him of a job in South Africa. A law firm there was seeking a lawyer with knowledge of English and **Gujarati** to communicate with a client. Although the work was low-paying and more secretarial than legal, Gandhi had few career options. He departed for South Africa without a family that had grown to include his wife and two children. It was there that he began his fight against injustice and racism.

A twelfth-century statue of Vishnu, a Hindu deity, with two goddesses beside him. Hinduism shaped many of the choices Gandhi made in life.

CHAPTER TWO

British India and South Africa

Gandhi's life is inextricably linked to the history of Great Britain. Practically his whole life was spent in lands that were loyal to the British Crown. He was born in the British colony of India, educated in London, worked in South Africa—a dominion of the British Empire—and then returned to British India. Gandhi did live to see the end of British rule in India, but only for a short time. Less than six months after independence, he was assassinated.

A map of British India and the Indian states that owed allegiance to it

India

The **Indian subcontinent** has a long, rich history. The Indus Valley was the home of one of the earliest civilizations in the world—a fact that is a source of pride and national identity for many Indians today. In the approximately 4,700 years between the rise of this early civilization and the arrival of European colonists, countless Indian states rose and fell. Occasionally, the subcontinent was united under one ruler. More often than not, it was divided into competing empires and kingdoms. The people of the area were (and continue to be) quite diverse. They were not united by a common language or religion. Even today, there are twenty-two official languages in India, and most Indians do not grow up speaking Hindi—the **lingua franca**—at home.

Religious diversity is also a hallmark of the continent. Three major religions still practiced today—Hinduism, Buddhism, and Jainism—all began in India. Furthermore, the Muslim conquest of India, which took place between the twelfth and sixteenth centuries CE, spread Islam throughout the region. Islam supplanted Buddhism, the former religion of the majority, which is now almost entirely absent from the country. (It should be noted that today, nearly 80 percent of the population is Hindu.)

India and the West had some contact from early on in human history. Goods traveled between India and Europe, and this formed an important trade route and means of cultural exchange for thousands of years. In the fourth century BCE, Alexander the Great and his army reached India and fought an Indian army (which, interestingly, featured war elephants). But it was not until the 1500s that European powers began to arrive in force and rule over portions of India. Lured by the lucrative spice trade, they seized cities on the coast from which to manage their trading empires.

For the next three centuries, the Portuguese, Dutch, French, and British established trading posts, built forts, and conquered cities across India. At first, the European powers did not attempt to rule the entire subcontinent—they were content to force local states to sign over small pieces of land to support their trade networks. But eventually, the French and British became locked in a struggle to dominate the entire region.

The conflict between the French and British was precipitated by the decline of the Mughal Empire in India. Until this decline, the Europeans were content to profit

The Taj Mahal was built by a Mughal emperor to be a tomb for his wife.

off a stable India overseen by a local power. But as the Mughal Empire fragmented, smaller Indian states took shape. They came into conflict with one another, and they often sought aid from the Europeans on their doorsteps.

French and British agents in India were eager to aid the Indian states. Involvement in the conflict could result in personal riches if one's ally prevailed, and an intense rivalry between France and Britain was set into motion. Ultimately, this resulted in open war on Indian soil between the two European powers and various Indian allies. Between 1746 and 1763, three separate Carnatic Wars were waged between France and Britain. (The Carnatic is a region of coastal India.) Two of these wars corresponded to times of open warfare between the European powers in Europe, while the third was a **proxy war** fought primarily by Indian allies.

During the Third Carnatic War, which coincided with the French and Indian War in North America, the British scored a decisive victory over the French and their allies at the Battle of Plassey. A force of just three thousand men led by a British colonel routed an army of fifty thousand men. The victory led to the overthrow of the ruler of Bengal—a key ally of France. Britain was able to secure Bengal, the richest state in India, for itself, and British **hegemony** in India was ensured. It was a turning point in history, one that would shape India's future for centuries to come.

Company Rule

With the end of the Third Carnatic War, Britain was the principal power of India. However, it was not the British government that ruled the region, but the East India Company—a private company owned by shareholders. The East India Company had its own private armies and navies and governed with absolute authority over its domain. It is important to mention that the company did not directly control much of India. Not only did some areas still belong to other European powers, but much of the region was ruled by Indian states that had a great deal of authority despite being subordinate to the East India Company. Local rulers would pass laws and collect taxes on behalf of the company.

At first, the East India Company tried to avoid further conflict in the region. Already the preeminent power, the British were content to profit peacefully. Yet over time, ambitious British leaders extended their control across almost all of India (with the exception of isolated areas still controlled by other European powers). Eventually, virtually all of present-day India, Sri Lanka, Pakistan, and Myanmar, as well as parts of Nepal and Afghanistan, would come under the control of Great Britain.

Company rule in India was harsh. The primary concern of the company was extracting money from the region to distribute to its shareholders in Europe. The plight of the people of India who lived under their dominion was largely ignored. When a famine swept through Bengal in 1770—killing a staggering ten million people—the company did not send food aid nor even lower taxes in the region. Even British officials back home began to question the company's methods.

One of the most famous men of the East India Company was Robert Clive. His meteoric rise—and fall—illustrates the brutal methods of the company he worked for. Born into a family of modest means in England, he went to work for the East India Company as a young man. At first, he did office work, but when the First Carnatic War broke out, he received an officer's commission in the private army of the company. He was involved in all three Carnatic Wars in a military capacity. He led British troops at the Battle of Plassey, and his exploits in battle put a huge swath of India under company rule.

Clive himself emerged from the Third Carnatic War an incredibly wealthy man. The treasury of Bengal was seized from its former ruler and put into the coffers of the company, but more than a little disappeared into Clive's personal fortune. He returned to Britain with more than $30 million in today's US dollars. It was a fortune that raised eyebrows in Britain—where many members of Parliament were shareholders of the company and wondered whether his newfound wealth ought to be in *their* pockets.

In 1772, the practices of the East India Company were debated in Parliament on the recommendation of the king. According to nineteenth-century historians Charles MacFarlane and Thomas Thomson, this was because:

> “*Few men not holders of India stock could reconcile themselves to the anomaly presented [by the East India Company], nor possibly conceive how a dozen or two of plain citizens called directors, and some hundreds of shareholders called proprietors, could be competent to the management of 15,000,000 of people at the distance of many thousands of miles.*

The East India Company was coming under increasing scrutiny that began to focus in on Robert Clive, whose personal fortune made him a lightning rod of criticism regarding corruption in India. Clive spoke in Parliament on his own behalf, and he managed to avoid any serious censure. However, his reputation was ruined and his health was failing. He committed suicide a few months after the parliamentary inquiry exonerated him. The boy who had “arrived at Madras in 1743 at the age of seventeen, poor, awkward, and without connexions,” according to Namier and Brooke’s *History of Parliament*, died one of the richest self-made men in Europe. However, his legacy—like that of the company he worked for—is tainted by prioritizing profits over the lives of Indians and basic human rights. The East India Company would outlive Clive by eighty-four years before it too came to end.

The Indian Rebellion of 1857

Discontent gradually grew in India under company rule. Taxes were burdensome, and British officials instituted

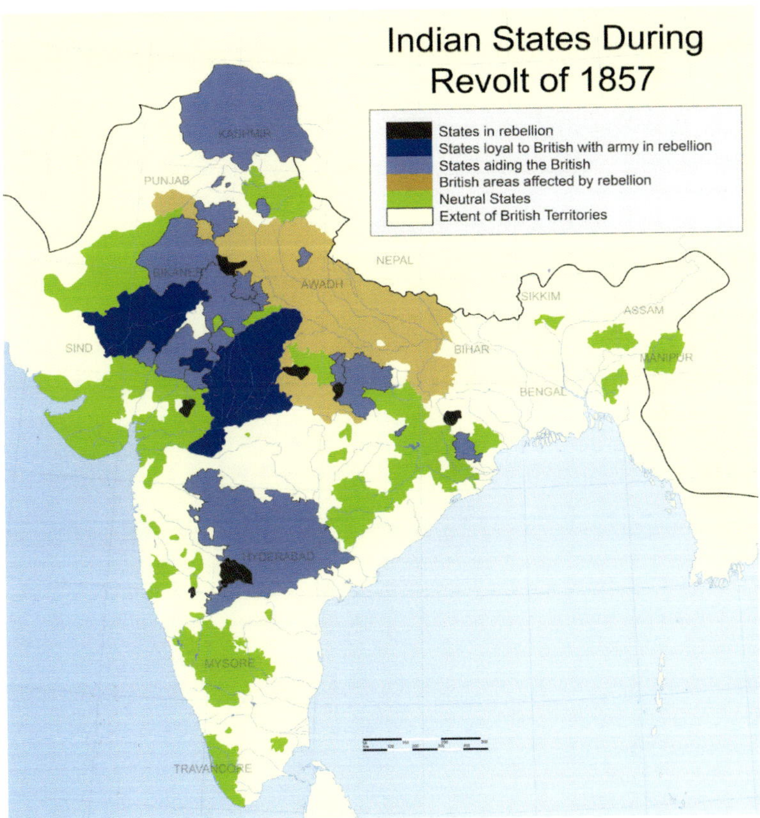

The Indian Rebellion of 1857 divided the Indian states. Some remained loyal to the crown, while others did not.

reforms that were deeply unpopular and angered the populace. One of the most important was the so-called Doctrine of Lapse. Adopted children of Indian rulers were forbidden from inheriting the throne according to this doctrine. As a result, the East India Company gradually absorbed the princely states of India as rulers died who failed to have a natural heir. There was no basis in Indian tradition or law for this reform: its principal reason was simply to consolidate power under the company over time and enrich the British. Princes loyal to the company were arbitrarily stripped of their lands and wealth after death if they were unlucky enough not to have an heir. It was an outrage that was hard to overlook for the people of India.

In 1857, the company went even further and simply annexed a state in northern India by the name of Oudh because the capability of its ruler was questioned. It was a decision that would have lasting consequences. At the time, there were 232,000 Indian soldiers in India and just 45,000 European soldiers. Furthermore, the majority of the soldiers of the army of Bengal—the largest army—were from Oudh.

At the same time, there was another crisis brewing. The Indian soldiers (known as sepoys) were issued with new rifles. In order to load the rifles, it was necessary to rip a paper cartridge of gunpowder open with one's teeth. The paper cartridge was greased with an unknown substance that likely contained tallow, which is fat from pigs and cows. The was an affront to both Hindus, who were forbidden from eating cows, and Muslims, who considered pigs unclean. The army responded by providing ungreased cartridges and allowing soldiers to grease the paper themselves, but the seeds of doubt were planted in the minds of the sepoys. A rumor spread that the paper itself contained animal fat due to its dark appearance and thickness. It was untrue, but the soldiers did not know.

The sepoys of the army of Bengal, already angered by the annexation of their home of Oudh, rose up in rebellion. Unit after unit killed their British officers and then marched on the city of Delhi. The limited number of European soldiers in the region were unable to stop them. The rebellion spread across much of northern India, and landowners and peasants in some areas lent their support to the soldiers. Some atrocities were committed against British civilians during the rebel advance, and the British press covered these in detail. When British soldiers finally turned the tide of the war, they repaid the atrocities in kind. Indian civilians were massacred in large numbers in areas that were retaken. Eventually, the rebellion was stamped out, but not before hundreds of thousands had died at great cost to the British Empire and East India Company.

The British government's faith in the company was finally exhausted. The company was dissolved, and a British colonial administration was put in place—the British Raj.

Two-fifths of the Indian subcontinent remained under the rule of Indian princes who were subordinate allies to the British. During what came to be known as the Sepoy Mutiny, many of these princes had remained loyal to the British while rebellion raged across northern India.

The British Raj

The new royal government of India tried to chart a new course for British dominion in India. It stopped deposing Indian rulers and paid more attention to conservative Indian values. In 1877, Queen Victoria was declared empress of India amid efforts to make British rule more palatable to the people of India. Railway and irrigation projects were sponsored across India to show the more

Like many other Indian monarchs, the maharaja of Mysore ruled his kingdom independently but was loyal to the British Raj.

benevolent side of British domination, and schools and universities opened across the region.

Nevertheless, many Indians were still not content with British rule. In 1885, the Indian National Congress was founded as a secular political party. It lobbied for increased political power for educated Indians under the British Raj. It was an important moment in Indian history. The congress organized opposition to British rule and laid the groundwork for later moves toward independence.

For the first twenty years of its existence, the congress did not seek outright independence from Great Britain. It simply wanted greater autonomy within the British Empire. But this gradually changed. In 1905, the sprawling province of Bengal (with nearly twice the population of England) was partitioned by the British **viceroy**. The Bengali people, who all spoke the same language, were distributed between two different provinces. Furthermore, the predominantly Muslim East was separated from the predominantly Hindu West. Many Indians immediately doubted the motives of the viceroy. The partition was supposed to allow the neglected eastern province to receive more attention from the government. However, the division of the Bengalis along religious lines raised suspicions that the viceroy was trying to encourage conflict among the local Indians to prevent their unified striving for independence.

After the partition, the Indian National Congress began to demand extensive political reform and, in later years, complete independence. With Gandhi at its helm, it would secure the long dreamed of independence for India decades later and would go on to be the most powerful political party in modern India.

Cape Colony

In 1488, Bartolomeu Dias—a Portuguese explorer—was the first European to reach South Africa. He was searching for a sea route to Asia to set up a new trade route. Unlike later explorers such as Columbus who sailed across the Atlantic looking for Asia, Dias was going the right way. He discovered the Cape of Good Hope at the southern tip of the African continent. This was the most direct way to Asia. While Dias never completed the journey, only ten years later another Portuguese explorer—Vasco da Gama—finally reached India. He brought two shiploads of spices back to Europe with him and helped spur the Age of Exploration.

The trip around Africa to Asia took approximately six months to complete. Ships had to stop along the way to resupply. As a result, the Portuguese and later colonial powers began setting up trading posts and forts along the coast of Africa. They served as resupply stops for ships as well as important nodes in the slave trade. Europeans would gather slaves at the forts, where ships would then take them to the Americas. This was the first step in the colonization of Africa and Asia. At this time, the Europeans were interested only in small settlements to support their trading ventures, but this would soon change.

In 1652, the first major European settlement was founded in South Africa. The Dutch East India Company stationed some employees at modern-day Cape Town in South Africa. Close to the Cape of Good Hope, this site was an ideal location: there was a natural bay, and the land was able to support large farms. The Dutch Cape Colony, as it came to be known, gradually expanded from this settlement to neighboring lands. Many of the settlers were former employees of the Dutch East India Company, but other Europeans also came for a new start.

The land was sparsely inhabited before the arrival of the Europeans. The Khoekhoe and San peoples who lived there used only stone tools, and they were driven out of the region by the expanding Dutch colony. The settlers imported slaves from other regions of Africa—and from Asia—to work on their plantations in the colony. Slavery and plantations were the bedrock of the local economy for more than a hundred years.

In 1795, the British invaded Cape Colony and seized it from the Dutch as part of a larger European struggle. The newly founded French Republic was at war with many of the monarchies of Europe. It had successfully conquered the Netherlands—and, as a result, its colonies around the world. In response, the British took the important Cape Colony from the Dutch. At the end of the war, they gave it back to the Dutch before once again seizing it during the Napoleonic Wars a couple years later. This time, the British would not give it back to the Dutch after the war. They kept the strategically located colony for themselves after Napoleon's defeat.

Afrikaners and Boers

In the years before the British took control of the colony, a unique cultural identity sprang up in South Africa. The white colonists and their descendants largely came from Western Europe. The Dutch made up the largest group, but there were also many German and French settlers. Over time, these colonists began to see themselves as Africans rather than Europeans. They referred to themselves as Afrikaners—the Dutch word for Africans. They spoke what we now call Afrikaans, a language descended from Dutch with some additions from the diverse group of people who also called Cape Colony home. Words from native African languages, other European languages, and Asian languages the slaves spoke all found their way into Afrikaans.

At first, most Afrikaners lived in Cape Town. Yet there was limited farmland and pastureland around the town, and the heavy-handed colonial administration bred discontent. Some chose to move farther afield. Pushing the native Africans off of their lands, they founded huge farms and imported slaves to work them. These farmers were soon called Boers (the Dutch word for farmers). A subgroup of Afrikaners, Boers were often considered even more independent and critical of the colonial administration than their brethren in Cape Town.

The Boers were a diverse group. Some operated large farms with slave labor. They produced wine and grains to sell on a grand scale. Others were trekboers, nomads who raised cattle and traveled the countryside in search of pastures. These trekboers were largely responsible for the expansion of Cape Colony. As they sought out better grazing land (and tried to move out of the authority of the colonial administration), the Dutch expanded the borders of the colony to keep up with them.

The Great Trek

With the advent of British rule, life for Afrikaners began to change. In 1807, the British abolished the slave trade in Cape Colony. The Afrikaners protested fiercely, and tension over race relations and slavery continued to fester in Cape Colony. The Afrikaners and British often found themselves at odds with one another, and ultimately the British recognized the right of black Africans to sue Afrikaners, much to their dismay.

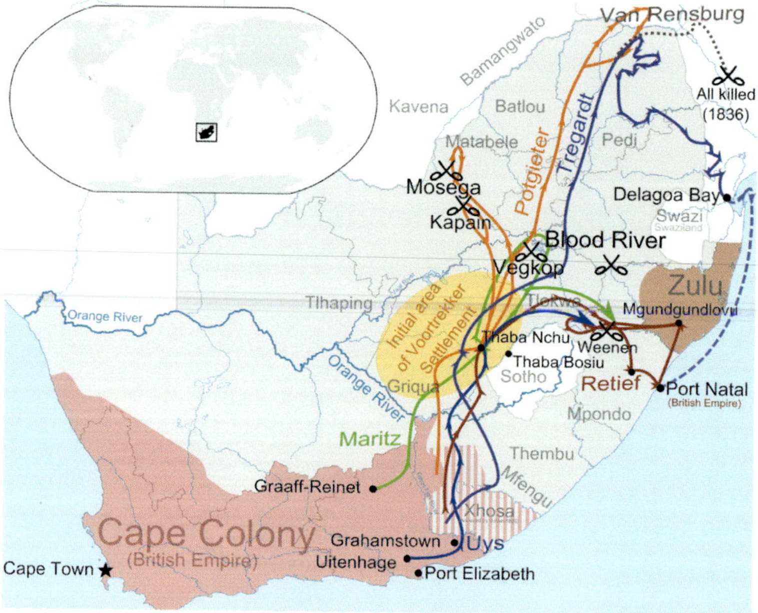

This map shows the routes groups of Boers took during the Great Trek and the battles they fought against the indigenous inhabitants.

A large influx of British colonists to the colony also fueled tensions. Some five thousand arrived in 1820, and more followed. Many Afrikaners felt that they were under threat by the British administration and colonists. In 1827, it was decreed that the official language of the colony would be English instead of Dutch. Many independent-minded Afrikaners were angered by these changes.

The last straw came in 1834. The Slavery Abolition Bill of 1833—passed in Great Britain and coming into effect a year later—abolished slavery in Cape Colony and most of the British Empire. For Boers with large farms, this was a massive economic loss. They would have to pay their laborers more. And while most trekboers owned few slaves, the loss of even a single slave for them was often devastating. Already poor and on the margins of the colony, they depended on free labor for their livelihood.

As a result, in 1835 more than twelve thousand Boers packed up their belongings and migrated out of Cape Colony, farther into Africa. It became known as the Great Trek and lasted for more than a decade. Groups of Boers journeyed through the interior of Africa, looking for new lands to settle on. They came into violent conflict with native Africans (such as the Zulus) over land and the kidnapping of Africans into slavery.

Eventually, the Boers set up their own states. The first one, the Natalia Republic, was quickly annexed by the British and became the Colony of Natal. But the later ones, the Transvaal and the Orange Free State, were recognized as independent by the British during the 1850s. The Great Trek had resulted in the Boer Republics, which would play a part in the history of the region and Gandhi's time in South Africa.

Diamonds and War

Tensions in southern Africa heated up in the following decades as diamonds and gold were discovered in the region. In 1867, diamonds were found at Kimberley—claimed by both the British and Boers. Eventually, the

Zulu warriors like these delivered a stinging defeat to the British Empire at the Battle of Isandlwana.

British won out and annexed the area. At the same time, the Boers were coming under increased pressure from the neighboring Zulu Kingdom. After years of Boer encroachment on their lands, it appeared the Zulus were going to fight back. The Transvaal accepted annexation by the British in 1877 to ensure their protection from the Zulus and other indigenous groups.

The British demanded the Zulus disband their army. When they did not, a British army invaded their territory and began the Anglo-Zulu War of 1879. The first major engagement of the war—the Battle of Isandlwana—was a disaster for the British. Shockingly, Zulu warriors armed with spears and shields were able to defeat a British column armed with rifles and artillery. More than a thousand British troops perished in the battle, along with a slightly smaller number of Zulu warriors. It was an embarrassing loss for the most powerful empire in the world. However, the British soon won the war and ensured security for the people of the Transvaal.

Unfortunately for the British, the Transvaal then decided that there was no reason to remain under British control with the Zulus defeated. They declared independence in 1880 and sparked the First Boer War. British troops tried to suppress the rebellion but failed. Boer forces heavily outnumbered the British in the area. Furthermore, the Boers were highly skilled marksmen since many were outdoorsmen and experienced hunters. The British were defeated in a series of battles and forced to sign a peace treaty granting the Transvaal its independence. For the first time since the American Revolution, the British army was defeated by one of its colonies.

However, in 1886 gold was discovered on the Witwatersrand—a ridge in the Transvaal. Tensions in the region rose as foreigners rushed into the Transvaal to make their fortune. The British watched enviously from the sidelines. Some British colonial administrators supported a raid to start a rebellion in the Transvaal against the Boer government. The raid failed but contributed to even more distrust between the two sides. In 1899, war broke out when the Transvaal demanded that British troops move

JAN SMUTS

Perhaps the most famous South African of Gandhi's era was Jan Smuts. Smuts was a military man turned politician. He fought with the Boers against the British during the Boer War. Then, during World War I and World War II, he fought on the side of the British against Germany, first as a general and then as a field marshal. He has the distinction of being the only person to sign the treaties that ended both world wars.

As a result of his distinguished military career, Smuts was a powerful politician. He served as the second prime minister of the Union of South Africa and also held important government positions at other times. He was the government's primary point of contact for Gandhi during his protests; Smuts defended the unjust acts that Gandhi was combating.

Gandhi's opinion of Smuts was mixed. He opined that Smuts "ranked as the ablest leader in South Africa, and today he takes a high place among the politicians of the British Empire, and even of the world." But he also did not trust Smuts after repeated broken promises and unfulfilled deals. Gandhi's final estimation was that:

> *I often felt that the general belief in South Africa about General Smuts's cunning did him perhaps less than justice. I am however sure of two things. First, he has some principles in politics which are not quite immoral. Secondly, there is room in his politics for cunning and on occasions for perversion of truth.*

Nevertheless, Gandhi made a gift of a pair of sandals to Smuts when he left South Africa. Smuts wore them for many summers at his farm before returning them to Gandhi with a note reading in part, "I am not worthy to stand in the shoes of so great a man."

After Gandhi left South Africa, Smuts continued to ensure that there was no equality for blacks and Indians in South Africa. He helped pass an important bill in 1920 that established segregation in residential areas. This was the groundwork for the later policy of apartheid—the strict racial segregation of all aspects of South African society which took shape in 1948 and lasted until 1991.

away from its borders and the British refused. The Second Boer War would last nearly three years and devastate the region. Although the British soon defeated the Boers on the battlefield, the men of both the Transvaal and the Orange Free State engaged in a protracted guerrilla war. The British responded by interning hundreds of thousands of civilians in concentration camps—tens of thousands died from disease and malnutrition.

In 1902, the war ended with the British victorious. The Transvaal and the Orange Free State became colonies of the British Empire. Eight years later, in 1910, the former Boer Republics and Cape Colony were joined together in the Union of South Africa—the predecessor of modern South Africa. The Boer Republics were no more. However, one of the major issues that had led to their creation—the treatment of black Africans—would remain a source of conflict in the region.

The Decline of the British Empire

When Gandhi was born in 1869, the British Empire was unquestionably the world's most powerful nation. Called "the empire on which the sun never sets," it sprawled across the globe. At its height, it covered nearly a quarter of the globe and ruled a quarter of the world's population. But its hegemony did not last. Although it came out of World War II victorious, it crumbled quickly over the two decades after the war's end. The United States and Soviet Union replaced it as the world's superpowers. The largest blow it suffered was the 1947 loss of India—the so-called jewel in the crown of the empire.

The decline did not stop there. Over the next two decades, Great Britain lost its African colonies. Bloody conflicts in Kenya and Egypt resulted in the deaths of thousands of African civilians and could not stop the inevitable. In 1997, the city of Hong Kong was given over to China, and the end of the empire was complete. Few overseas territories remained under British control, and those that did were sparsely inhabited, such as the Falkland Islands in South America.

The empire that shaped Gandhi's life had come to an end. However, its legacy can still be seen around the world today. English is spoken across the globe both as a majority language, such as in Australia, and as an official language that the majority of people do not speak, such as in Sierra Leone. In many countries, courts and universities still operate in English due to their colonial history.

Gandhi converses with Jawaharlal Nehru, who later became the first prime minister of India, during their struggle for independence.

CHAPTER THREE

Nonviolent Resistance

Gandhi's nonviolent resistance began in the country of South Africa. He would refine his personal philosophy there and master the means of protest and resistance. Once he had achieved his aims there, he returned home to India and challenged British rule. Were it not for his experiences in South Africa, Gandhi might never have risen to become the famous figure that he is today.

The Decision to Resist

Gandhi arrived in the South African port city of Durban in 1893. He was met at the dock by an employee of the law firm named Abdulla Sheth. It was immediately clear to Gandhi that Sheth, and all others of Indian descent, were treated as second-class citizens. Though he was a successful merchant, Sheth was not given much respect by white South Africans. When Sheth took Gandhi to court one day so that he could see it, the judge ordered Gandhi to remove his turban. Rather than comply, Gandhi stood up and walked out of the court.

It was his first act of nonviolent resistance against an oppressive state, but it would not be his last. He later toyed with the idea of simply replacing his turban with an English-style hat to avoid problems in the future, but it was Abdulla Sheth who convinced him not to, as a matter of patriotism and pride. The incident in court was reported on in the local newspaper at the time. Having just arrived in South Africa, Gandhi had already achieved some notoriety as a dissident.

Soon, it was time for Gandhi to depart the coastal city of Durban for Pretoria—the inland administrative capital. He boarded the first-class train compartment in Durban. At first, nothing was amiss. However, another passenger soon passed by and saw Gandhi sitting in his compartment. He protested to the railway attendant that a "colored" man was sitting in first class. The attendant ordered Gandhi to gather his things and leave first class, but Gandhi refused because he had purchased a first-class ticket and had already been allowed to sit there. The attendant threatened to have a constable forcibly eject Gandhi from the train, and when Gandhi still refused to move, this is exactly what happened.

Gandhi found himself in the small railway station of Pietermaritzburg, with no other trains departing until the next day. High in the mountains, the temperature dropped quite low overnight as Gandhi huddled in the waiting room, too afraid of harassment to even ask for his coat that was in his luggage, which was held by the train company.

That cold night in the mountains of South Africa, Gandhi resolved to fight injustice in South Africa rather than flee from it. It was a momentous decision that would shape the history of the twentieth century. Gandhi wrote about this important time in his autobiography years later:

“

I began to think of my duty. Should I fight for my rights or go back to India, or should I go on to Pretoria without minding the insults, and return to India after finishing the case? It would be cowardice to run back to India without fulfilling my obligation. The hardship to which I was subjected was superficial—only a symptom of the deep disease of color prejudice. I should try, if possible, to root out the disease and suffer hardships in the process. ***Redress*** *for wrongs*

I should seek only to the extent that would be necessary for the removal of the color prejudice.

For the next twenty years, he lived in South Africa and fought against the prejudice he experienced that day.

Early Years in South Africa

A year after the fateful night in Pietermaritzburg, Gandhi founded the Natal Indian Congress. It was named after the Indian National Congress, which Gandhi admired, and it sought to protect the rights of Indians across Natal.

Gandhi (*center, back row*) poses with the other founders of the Natal Indian Congress.

It quickly garnered a large number of members, with Gandhi at their helm.

A task that preoccupied Gandhi during this time was the collection of money from congress members. Yearly dues were required of all members, and well-off Indians were expected to pay more than the minimum. However, after the initial enthusiasm for the new organization wore off, many community members were hesitant to pay their dues. Consequently, Gandhi traveled about the countryside in person to collect and fund the congress's activities. On one occasion, a wealthy merchant refused to pay the full amount he owed. Worried such incidents would become commonplace if he backed down, Gandhi sat outside the man's house all night and refused to eat. The next morning, the man finally gave in and paid the full amount, as well as hosting a meal for Gandhi and his companions. It was the first time Gandhi would refuse to eat to further his ends; it was a mark of things to come.

The Natal Indian Congress worked on a variety of issues that affected Indians of all classes. One important issue in these early years was a proposed tax on indentured servants. At the time, many Indians in South Africa came to the country in indentured servitude. They were needed to work the sugar plantations, but they were never welcomed warmly in their new home. Their condition was often compared to that of slaves for the duration of their five-year contract. If they left their masters, they were imprisoned, and what few rights they had under the law were often ignored in practice.

One benefit indentured servitude offered was that those who completed their five-year contract could remain in the country. There, they often had some economic opportunity and could look forward to buying a small plot of land. However, in 1894, the South African government decided this was to be discouraged. They disapproved of former indentured servants settling in the country and competing in agriculture and trade with native South Africans. To decrease the likelihood that former indentured servants would stay, they proposed an annual poll tax of £25 (equal to more than $3,000 in 2017) for those who remained in the country after their five-year contract without signing a new contract of servitude.

It was an outrageous amount of money. The typical servant made at most 14 shillings a month—£8.4 a year (there are twenty shillings in a pound). Even a single man could not afford to pay his own tax based on his salary as a laborer, let alone the tax of a wife and children.

Gandhi and the Natal Indian Congress lobbied tirelessly for the proposed tax to be abandoned. In the end, the government agreed to reduce it to £3 a year—still more than a third of a laborer's salary. It was a small victory for the congress, but also a disappointment that any tax was levied.

In 1896, Gandhi's law contract in South Africa came to an end. He prepared to depart for India and went to a farewell party thrown by his employer. At the party, Gandhi learned of a new proposed bill to **disenfranchise** Indians in Natal. The partygoers implored Gandhi to stay in South Africa and lead the fight against this new injustice. Gandhi agreed, but first he decided to return to India. There, he tried to raise support for the cause of Indians in South Africa, and he also secured transportation for his wife and children to come join him in Africa.

The Lynch Mob

When he returned to South Africa, news of his work in India preceded him. White South Africans believed that Gandhi was slandering their country by spreading word of its injustices abroad. A white mob soon pursued Gandhi through the streets of Durban. They beat and harassed him, only stopping when the wife of the police superintendent came to his aid and shielded him by walking next to him. This gave the police time to send an armed escort to take him to his friend's house, where he was headed. However, that night the mob came back. It surrounded the house and demanded Gandhi be turned over so that he could be lynched. The police superintendent was sympathetic to Gandhi's plight but also completely unable to check the anger of the mob. He sent word to Gandhi that he must escape immediately in a police uniform or else he would surely die that night—there was talk of burning the house down with everyone in it.

Gandhi heeded his advice and fled. The superintendent told the mob Gandhi was gone, but they did not believe him. He was forced to take men from the mob on a search of the house to prove Gandhi was not there so that they did not set it alight with Gandhi's family and his friend's family inside.

Gandhi refused to press charges against any members of the mob. As part of his nonviolent philosophy, he had decided that he would never seek legal redress for personal injuries, only societal injustices.

The Boer War

Over the next years, Gandhi remained active in the Indian community in South Africa. When the Boer War broke out in 1899, there was some question among Indians regarding how to react. It did not appear to be their war to fight in; the grievances were between the Boers and the British. Furthermore, there was concern that any involvement might come back to haunt the Indian community if they supported the losing side.

However, Gandhi believed that it was not possible for Indians to stay aloof. He later recorded his feelings at the time about the conflict:

“

I felt that, if I demanded rights as a British citizen, it was also my duty, as such, to participate in the defense of the British Empire. I held then that India could achieve her complete emancipation only within and through the British Empire.

In light of this conviction, Gandhi set about organizing an ambulance corps to aid the British army. He led more than a thousand Indians during the war as they transported

Members of the Natal Indian Ambulance Corps, which Gandhi founded

wounded soldiers. They were supposed to operate behind the front lines; however, on one occasion their services were necessary on the field of battle. Given the choice as to whether they would face personal danger to aid the wounded, Gandhi and his men rushed onto the battlefield without a second thought. Gandhi and a number of other men in his command received medals for their bravery.

It was Gandhi's hope that their service in the war would result in more rights for Indians after the war. Disappointingly, this did not come to pass. The rights of Indians in South Africa were constantly threatened and curtailed by the government, even after their brave service.

Communal Living

In 1904, two years after the war ended, Gandhi founded the Phoenix Settlement about 15.5 miles (25 kilometers) from Durban. From the settlement, he published and printed the *Indian Opinion*, a newspaper that covered the issues related to the lives of Indians in South Africa. Gandhi and his family, as well as other people who worked on the newspaper, lived together on a large farm in separate houses. It was the first community that he established, and it would be one of many.

Several years later, after the first Satyagraha campaign, Gandhi founded the Tolstoy Farm in South Africa. The great Russian writer Leo Tolstoy was a leading intellectual of the time and a fierce proponent of pacifism. He had published "A Letter to a Hindu" in 1909, urging nonviolent resistance to British rule in India. Gandhi wrote him afterward and asked permission to translate Tolstoy's work into Gujarati so that more Indians could read it. Tolstoy happily agreed, and the two men corresponded over the next year until Tolstoy passed away in 1910. In their letters, they discussed the situation of Indians in South Africa.

Tolstoy Farm was a progressive attempt to put many of Tolstoy's and Gandhi's ideals into action in South Africa. Boys and girls were educated together on the farm—something virtually unheard of at the time—and every effort was made to promote the moral development of the students. All residents at the farm, nearly one hundred people, worked and did chores, regardless of their station in life. The farm, founded in 1910, was also the headquarters from which many of Gandhi's later Satyagraha campaigns were led.

The First Satyagraha Campaign

In 1906, the Asiatic Law Amendment Ordinance was passed in the Transvaal. It later became known as the Black Act. It required all Indians to register with the police and have their fingerprints taken as if they were criminals. They then had to carry a certificate of registration with them at all times detailing their personal information. At any time, they could be stopped on the street and asked to provide their registration certificate. If they failed to do so, they could be fined or imprisoned. The police were even allowed to go into the homes of Indians and those of Indian descent to inspect their certificates if they desired to do so. It was an oppressive law that singled out Indians for humiliation.

In response to the passing of the Black Act, Gandhi called for a meeting of Indian leaders in the Transvaal. He translated the words of the act into Gujarati and explained the importance of the situation to them:

> "
>
> *This is a very serious crisis. If the Ordinance were passed and if we acquiesced in it, it would be imitated all over South Africa. As it seems to me, it is designed to strike at the very root of our existence in South Africa. It is not the last step, but the first step with a view to hounding us out of the country. We are therefore responsible for the safety, not only of the ten or fifteen thousand Indians in the Transvaal but of the entire Indian community in South Africa. Again, if we fully understand all the implications of this legislation, we shall find that India's honor is in our keeping. For the Ordinance seeks to humiliate*

not only ourselves but also the motherland. The humiliation consists in the degradation of innocent men. No one will take it upon himself to say that we have done anything to deserve such legislation. We are innocent, and insult offered to a single innocent member of a nation is tantamount to insulting the nation as a whole.

Gandhi and his compatriots tried to convince the government to scrap the new law, but their efforts failed. Gandhi responded by organizing his first Satyagraha campaign. He urged fellow Indians to refuse to register with the police, be fingerprinted, or carry their registration card with them. The registration offices were picketed by Gandhi's supporters. When the law came into effect in 1907, just 511 Indians had registered out of a population of some 13,000.

The South African government did not take this act of nonviolent resistance lightly. It imprisoned Indians who had not registered, including Gandhi in 1908. However, the jails were soon full, and the prisoners were still unwilling to back down. Jan Smuts negotiated an end to the conflict with Gandhi. If the Indians agreed to register, the government would repeal the law. Gandhi agreed and was released from prison. On his way to register, Gandhi was beaten violently by fellow Indians who thought he had betrayed the movement and surrendered.

Smuts later reneged on his agreement with Gandhi, and the Black Act remained in effect. In response, Gandhi organized a massive protest where Indians who had registered burned their cards publicly.

The Indian Relief Act

For nearly a decade, Gandhi continued leading Satyagraha campaigns in South Africa. In addition to the Black Act, he and his supporters also challenged a law that restricted the movement of Indians between the states of Natal and Transvaal. Indians pointedly walked across the border, daring the authorities to arrest them when their prisons were already overflowing. At the height of the campaign, in 1913, Gandhi led a group of two thousand people across the border to publicize the issue.

Finally, in 1914, the South African government came to the negotiating table. The crisis had tarnished their reputation internationally, and Gandhi's supporters continued to fill prisons around the country, refusing to follow the unjust laws. The Indian Relief Act of 1914 abolished the £3 poll tax, freed Indian protesters from prison, and allowed Indians freedom of movement throughout the country. It was a stunning victory for Gandhi and an affirmation of the effectiveness of Satyagraha.

Gandhi's work in South Africa was finally complete. The same year, he left South Africa and set sail for India.

Miners in South Africa strike during Gandhi's Satyagraha.

He took with him his strategy of Satyagraha and the lessons he had learned about nonviolent resistance in South Africa. The government of South Africa was elated to see him go. Smuts remarked, "The saint has left our shores. I sincerely hope forever."

India at Last

Gandhi received a hero's welcome in India. His work in South Africa had not gone unnoticed, and honors were heaped upon him. At first, he did not enter Indian politics. His political mentor Gopal Krishna Gokhale asked Gandhi to promise that he would not take a political stance for his first year in India. Instead, he should observe his homeland after his long absence and make up his mind about what to do next. Gandhi agreed, and although Gokhale—a leading member of the Indian National Congress—soon passed away, Gandhi kept his promise.

Gandhi founded the Sabarmati **Ashram** outside the town of Ahmadabad, Gujarat, in 1915. It would play an important role in the upcoming fight for Indian independence, and Gandhi lived there for the next fifteen years. In the beginning, twenty-five people lived on its grounds, but this number soon grew. Life at the ashram was simple and communal. Everyone ate together in a communal dining hall and did their part in daily chores. Like at the Phoenix Farm before it, social equality played a large part in Gandhi's vision of the ashram. He went out of his way to ensure that an untouchable family joined the community, even though other members objected.

In 1917, Gandhi began to take a more active role in Indian politics. He visited the regions of Champaran and Kheda. There, he led his first Satyagraha campaigns in India. He organized peasant resistance against unfair treatment by landlords. During the campaign, Gandhi was arrested but was almost immediately freed. The government realized that imprisoning him would worsen the situation. In the end, Gandhi's campaign worked, and laws were passed to protect peasants in the regions from further abuses. It was a much smaller campaign than Gandhi's later actions in India but an important early step nonetheless. It also marked the beginning of Gandhi's outreach to Indian peasants. Until Gandhi's arrival in India, the independence movement had largely been restricted to the middle and upper classes.

The Amritsar Massacre

In 1919, the Rowlatt Acts were passed in the British Raj. They allowed the government to imprison Indians without a trial if they were accused of terrorism and restricted the

Today, a monument memorializes the Amritsar Massacre.

freedom of the press. They were met with widespread condemnation and protest. The acts were a response to the growing independence movement in India, but instead of curbing the movement, they inflamed it.

Rioting and protests broke out across the country, especially in the north. In the city of Amritsar, a curfew had been instituted, and public gatherings were banned after local unrest. However, a crowd of more than a thousand demonstrators and pilgrims passing through the area gathered in the public garden Jallianwalla Bagh. A British contingent of soldiers responded and, without warning, fired into the crowd of unarmed civilians. When the smoke cleared, at least 379 people were dead, according to official sources—although the true number is likely much higher. The Amritsar Massacre, as it came to be known, served as a catalyst for more protests against British rule.

Noncooperation Movement

Gandhi was appalled by the passing of the Rowlatt Acts and the Amritsar Massacre that followed. In the months following the massacre, many British politicians lauded the actions of the military in Amritsar, and the officer in charge of troops there was cleared of wrongdoing. It was apparent that British rule in India could not be tolerated any longer.

In response, Gandhi launched the noncooperation movement in 1920. He sought **swaraj**—or self-rule—for India. It was his first nationwide Satyagraha campaign in India. He launched the campaign at the Nagpur conference of the Indian National Congress with widespread support. However, not everyone agreed with Gandhi's plan. Many moderate members thought that swaraj should result from lawful reform rather than nonviolent protest. Only one man dared to vote against Gandhi's plan out of the approximately fifty thousand people at the meeting—Mohammed Ali Jinnah, a Muslim political leader who would play a crucial role in the history of India and Pakistan, which Jinnah helped create. Jinnah was shouted down by Gandhi's supporters when he spoke out against the plan. He abandoned the Indian National Congress because of this response, and it was a sign of the discord to come in the Indian independence movement. In 1924, Gandhi became president of the Indian National Congress.

The noncooperation movement was based on a number of different kinds of protest. Indians boycotted English schools as well as English courts. Many prominent lawyers resigned rather than continue their practices in a public show of defiance. English goods, especially cloth, were also boycotted. Imported clothes were burned publicly in bonfires, and liquor stores were picketed across the country. The movement continued for more than a year, with demonstrations and protests

Bhagat Singh

Not all Indians agreed with Gandhi's insistence on ahimsa. Perhaps the most famous Indian independence fighter who turned to violence was Bhagat Singh. Born in Punjab (today part of Pakistan) in 1907, Singh was raised a Sikh. However, he was a voracious reader and abandoned the religion of his birth to become an atheist and socialist as a young adult. Even from a young age he was captivated by the struggle for Indian independence, and he soon devoted his life to this pursuit. He joined and later founded revolutionary organizations and vehemently opposed British rule in India.

In 1928, one of Singh's friends (and a prominent Indian leader), Lala Lajpat Rai, died after attending a protest march. He was struck by James A. Scott, a police superintendent, with a **lathi**, and he died several days later from a heart attack. Singh blamed the police superintendent for his death, although the British blamed it on Rai's advanced age and health problems. In retaliation, Singh and a companion gunned down the assistant police superintendent, mistaking him for Scott. Despite a manhunt, Singh evaded arrest and fled the city.

The next year, Singh and another man threw bombs into the Central Legislative Assembly while it was in session. Some lawmakers were injured, but none died. Singh and his companion did not attempt to flee and were arrested. They claimed that the bombing was not meant to kill anyone; instead, it was meant to give them a platform to spread their ideas. During the bombing, they had thrown leaflets into the hall that denounced British rule in India. They had also shouted "Inquilab Zindabad!" ("Long live the Revolution!"), and this became a rallying cry across India.

Singh was sentenced to death for his actions. While he awaited his execution, he went on a hunger strike to protest the treatment of other political prisoners. On March 23, 1931, he was hanged at the age of just twenty-three years old. Maligned as a terrorist by the British, he is considered a national hero in India today.

Gandhi was embroiled in controversy after Singh's death—a controversy that still lasts to this day. Some people believed that he could have done more to secure leniency for Singh and his fellow conspirators. Although Gandhi did petition the British to commute their death sentences, many younger revolutionaries doubted his sincerity in the venture. However, most historians believe Gandhi did his best to save Singh. Gandhi was a vocal critic of the death penalty and gained nothing from Singh's death.

taking place across the country. Gandhi traveled around India exhorting crowds to continue the campaign and burn their foreign clothes.

The British Raj seemed ungovernable, and its leaders were unsure how to react. At first, they tried to ignore the movement rather than increase tensions with a heavy-handed response. However, eventually they decided to change their response as the movement continued. They imprisoned tens of thousands of Indians, including most leaders (with the strategic exception of Gandhi). Gandhi responded by increasing the pressure against the government. He called for a renewed Satyagraha campaign focused on just one town to draw the world's attention there. But before the new campaign could commence, tragedy struck.

In the small village of Chauri Chaura, a crowd of demonstrators was fired on by the local police. The crowd reacted by rushing forward rather than back. The police panicked and fled into their station, which the enraged crowd set on fire. When the police tried to escape, they were cut down and thrown back into the burning station. Twenty-two policemen died in the violence.

Gandhi immediately called for an end to the noncooperation movement. The principle of ahimsa—or harmlessness—had been violated. He fasted for a number of days to do personal penance for his part in leading the movement that had resulted in such violence.

After the movement ended, Gandhi published two articles highly critical of British rule in India. He called for swaraj and, among other criticisms, called the British Raj "wholly evil." He was arrested and tried for sedition. Gandhi pled guilty to the charge, happy to admit he sought the end of the British Raj. He was sentenced to six years in prison, but he would serve less than two before being released following an operation on his appendix.

The Salt March

Between his release from prison in 1924 and 1930, Gandhi withdrew from the struggle for independence. He turned his attention to social issues and engaged in a number of different causes. One of his most important efforts was his attempt to ease the growing tensions between Muslims and Hindus in India. They had been united in their efforts during the noncooperation campaign, but in later years, cracks began to show in their unity. In 1924, a violent riot broke out that resulted in the deaths of more than a hundred people, mostly Hindus and Sikhs. Gandhi responded by going on a twenty-one-day fast for unity. It worked, and sectarian violence abated for a time, but the peace would not last.

Gandhi also confronted a number of other social issues of the time. He campaigned against child marriage and the marginalization of the untouchable caste. He also

Gandhi and his entourage walking during the Salt March

advocated for Indians to take up making their own cloth with a spinning wheel—both as a means to avoid purchasing foreign cloth and as a way to combat poverty and unemployment.

In 1930, Gandhi reentered the fight for independence in spectacular fashion. The Indian National Congress had declared independence on January 26, but India remained under the control of the British. To pressure the Raj, Gandhi launched a new Satyagraha: the Salt March. Gandhi and seventy-eight companions left his Sabarmati Ashram to march toward the sea. He declared his intent to manufacture his own salt from the seawater once he arrived. This was illegal at the time, as the British held a monopoly on salt production. Salt was an important source of revenue for the government, although paying for it placed a great burden on ordinary Indians. Many lived near the sea and were capable of making their own salt were it not for the British ban.

Gandhi stopped at villages along his 241-mile (388 km) journey. He delivered speeches to adoring crowds, urging them to make their own salt and spin their own cloth. In doing so, they would undermine the economic system of the British Raj. Finally, after weeks of intense media coverage and impassioned speeches, Gandhi arrived at the sea. He bent down and picked up a piece of salt from the beach, breaking the British law. Indians around the country followed his example and began producing their own salt. The government responded by imprisoning tens of thousands. Gandhi himself was arrested not long after reaching the coast, but his campaign was not finished yet.

Prior to his arrest, he organized a Satyagraha at the saltworks of Dharasana. The nonviolent protest was met with overwhelming force. The American journalist Webb Miller, who witnessed the events, wrote the following account:

“

> *Suddenly, at a word of command, scores of native police rushed upon the advancing marchers and rained blows on their heads with their steel-shod*

lathis. Not one of the marchers even raised an arm to fend off the blows. They went down like ten-pins. From where I stood I heard the sickening whacks of the clubs on unprotected skulls. The waiting crowd of watchers groaned and sucked in their breaths in sympathetic pain at every blow.

Those struck down fell sprawling, unconscious or writhing in pain with fractured skulls or broken shoulders. In two or three minutes the ground was quilted with bodies. Great patches of blood widened on their white clothes. The survivors without breaking ranks silently and doggedly marched on until struck down.

Although the Salt March did not bring about any concessions from the government, it inspired outrage around the globe over how Indians were being treated under the British. Gandhi was almost immediately released from prison by the British in an attempt to defuse the conflict. It was clear they had little insight into how to deal with the charismatic leader and his nonviolent followers.

Quit India

After the Salt March, Gandhi once again withdrew from the public politics of independence in favor of social issues.

The body of a killed protester is carried by his compatriots during the Quit India movement.

In 1939, World War II began, and Great Britain joined the war against Nazi Germany and the Empire of Japan. India was an important part of British war efforts, as well as a possible future scene of fighting as the armies of Japan swept across Asia. To ensure Indian loyalty, the British government sent the Cripps Mission to discuss the future of India after war.

Stafford Cripps met with the leaders of the Indian National Congress, including Gandhi, but the two sides could not come to an agreement. Cripps offered India the status of dominion—a small step up, but far from the self-rule that the Indian independence movement desired. With the failure of the Cripps Mission, Gandhi launched his final, nationwide Satyagraha: the Quit India movement.

On August 8, 1942, Gandhi called for an end to British rule in India. He said, "I am not going to be satisfied with anything short of complete freedom. We shall do or die. We shall either free India or die in the attempt." Marches and protests broke out across India as the people supported Gandhi. The British response crushed the movement. They arrested and imprisoned all the leaders of the Indian National Congress, including Gandhi, within twenty-four hours. Protesters were met with violence by the police. More than a thousand Indians were killed by the police crackdown, and the movement, with no leaders to direct it, came to an end.

Independence Day

Although Great Britain was one of the victors of World War II, the war made it plain for all to see that the heyday of the British Empire was at an end. It no longer had the resources to span the globe, and its colonies—like those of the French and other old colonial powers—were increasingly restless under its heavy-handed imperialism. Violence against independence movements was not only costly but also tarnished the reputation of the countries of Europe. The United States urged its ally to give India independence peacefully, rather than risk

Lord Mountbatten (*left*) meets with Mohammed Ali Jinnah (*center*), the future leader of Pakistan.

the country turning to the growing might of the Soviet Union in its search for independence.

In March of 1947, Lord Mountbatten, the last viceroy of India, arrived in the Raj. His mission was to quickly grant the country independence. In August of the same year, India and Pakistan were finally granted their independence. The British Raj was partitioned into these two states: one with a Muslim majority and one with a Hindu majority. The partition was a bitter blow to Gandhi, who had argued for a single independent state. However, the Muslim minority of the Raj were fully committed to partition. They feared that they would be marginalized and persecuted in a democratic India since they were greatly outnumbered by the Hindu majority. (The Sikh minority was largely ignored in the partition, given their small numbers.) India had gained its independence at last, but the violence between Hindus and Muslims in the region was just beginning. In the next chapter, we'll take a closer look at the partition and its effects, as well as Gandhi's wide-ranging influence.

Around the world, statues commemorate Gandhi and his achievements.

CHAPTER FOUR

Gandhi's Legacy

The legacy of Gandhi is multifaceted. He is held up as the paragon of nonviolence—or ahimsa, as he would have called it. Even during his life, this led to him being regarded as a saint. Many political movements and leaders have been inspired by this nonviolence, and the huge success that Gandhi found with it, and have copied his methods. Just two years after the devastation and unimaginable violence of World War II and the Holocaust came to an end, India gained its independence through Gandhi's focus on love, truth, and nonviolence. It was a powerful example for the world, and one that is still remembered and cherished to this day. Political leaders such as Nelson Mandela and Martin Luther King Jr. followed in the footsteps of Gandhi, demonstrating his influence far after his death.

But Gandhi's path of nonviolence is just part of his legacy. Perhaps the most tangible mark he left on the world was the creation of the independent states of India and Pakistan. His tireless campaigning for swaraj reshaped the map of the world. Without Gandhi, it is hard to say when India would have eventually gained independence—and how much more Indian and British blood would have been spilled in pursuit of it. But the early history of independent India and Pakistan was also the greatest defeat that Gandhi suffered. The partition of the two countries proved to be an event of extraordinary violence and chaos. The conflict at its root—between Muslims and Hindus in the Indian subcontinent—would lead to the assassination of Gandhi not long after Independence Day.

The Tragedy of Partition

The history of partition and who was responsible is still controversial to this day. Partition is the root of the current conflict between Pakistan and India, and therefore it is not just a matter of history but also of modern-day politics. The religious communities of India had long lived in peace, but that began to change on a large scale in 1946—the year before partition. On August 16, a day of rioting claimed

Refugees crowd onto trains during the chaos and mass migration following the partition of India and Pakistan.

the lives of thousands as Hindu and Muslim mobs clashed in the streets. It was the result of a planned peaceful protest by the Muslim League that soon went awry. Civilians were murdered by armed groups, and the country was shocked by the sectarian violence. This day convinced the British that partition was the only way forward.

But partition was also the result of personal conflicts at the highest level of Indian politics. By the 1940s, Gandhi and his close political ally Jawaharlal Nehru were at odds with the most influential Muslim leader, Mohammed Ali Jinnah (the future first governor-general of Pakistan). Their personal animosity was intense, and communication between the Hindu and Muslim leaders was confrontational. Jinnah had opposed many of Gandhi's Satyagraha campaigns and had drawn the ire of Gandhi's supporters as a result. The future leader of Pakistan was also deeply secular and frequently criticized Gandhi's religious approach to politics. The convergence of Hinduism and politics was viewed as threatening by the Muslim minority.

Gandhi argued forcefully that India should not be partitioned. He tried to mend ties with Jinnah and warned Indian politicians that partition would result in bloodshed. In one memorable quotation, Gandhi compares partition to vivisection—the dissection of a living creature:

"

To demand the vivisection of a living organism is to ask for its very life. It is a call to war. The Congress cannot be party to such a fratricidal war ... If you distrust the Congress, you may rest assured that there is to be a perpetual war

> *between the Hindus and the* ***Mussalmans****, and the country will be doomed to continue warfare and bloodshed. If such warfare is to be our lot, I shall not live to witness it.*

It was Jinnah and the Muslim League he led that insisted on partition as the British planned to withdraw. Nehru and the other leaders of the Indian National Congress agreed, against the advice of Gandhi, and partition became inevitable in the months before independence. It was left to the British to delineate the border between the two countries, and they hastily drew up a border that split the country in two. The border was not even revealed until days after independence. Inevitably, millions of Muslims found themselves in the new state of India, while millions of Sikhs and Hindus ended up in Pakistan. The religious communities were hopelessly intermingled in many areas of the former Raj.

The result was sectarian violence on an unprecedented scale, even as Jinnah and Nehru, the leaders of the two countries, made calls for religious freedom and restraint. Millions of Indians and Pakistanis packed up what belongings they could carry and set off—often on foot—for their new homeland, which could be hundreds of miles away. In the chaos, riots broke out in many cities across India, and civilians were murdered. The violence spread as grieving refugees who had lost friends and family arrived in new cities and took revenge. In all, between one million and two million Indians and Pakistanis died in the violence. Neighbors turned on neighbors, and the politicians of India and Pakistan were helpless to stop the violence. British police and soldiers still stationed in the country were unequipped to help.

During the violence, Gandhi called for calm. He began to fast in Kolkata (then called Calcutta)—the scene of the worst riots a year earlier—and said that he would continue to refuse food until he died unless the violence ended. As a result, widespread violence never broke out in Kolkata, one of the places most plagued by sectarian violence in the past. But Gandhi could do little to stop violence across the entire region.

In the end, some fifteen million people left or fled their former homes. It was one of the largest migrations in human history. The seeds of conflict were also sown between Pakistan and India. Princely states still existed throughout the Raj, and they were allowed to determine for themselves whether to join India or Pakistan. Unfortunately, the princely state of Jammu and Kashmir on the border of the two countries was led by a Hindu ruler but had a Muslim majority. This fact led to the Indo-Pakistani War of 1947—the first open conflict between the two nations but far from the last.

Today, the status of Jammu and Kashmir is still disputed by India and Pakistan. India controls the

The same year as India and Pakistan achieved independence, war broke out between the two countries.

majority of the territory, but it has a Muslim majority, and conflict between civilians and police occasionally flares up. Furthermore, the border itself is sometimes the scene of border skirmishes between India and Pakistan—as well as the site and cause of four wars between the two countries in the seventy years since independence.

Assassination

Gandhi also fell victim to the sectarian strife. He was killed not by a Muslim, but by a Hindu extremist who thought that he was too accommodating toward Muslims. On January 30, 1948, he was shot three times as he walked

Large crowds gathered for Gandhi's funeral.

through a crowd of people who had come to see him. The assassin was immediately apprehended.

Nehru—then the first prime minister of India—delivered a now famous radio address to the nation, eulogizing Gandhi:

“

The light has gone out of our lives and there is darkness everywhere. I do not know what to tell you and how to say it. Our beloved leader,

> ***Bapu*** *as we called him, the Father of the Nation, is no more. Perhaps I am wrong to say that. Nevertheless, we will never see him again as we have seen him for these many years. We will not run to him for advice and seek solace from him, and that is a terrible blow, not to me only, but to millions and millions in this country. And it is a little difficult to soften the blow by any other advice that I or anyone else can give you.*

Millions around the world mourned the great leader. However, the assassin himself was unrepentant. He tried to justify his actions in court: "I do say that my shots were fired at the person whose policy and action had brought rack and ruin and destruction to millions of Hindus." It was an argument that fell on deaf ears. He was hanged for his crime, despite the protests of Gandhi's family, who urged mercy.

Modern India

While the partition of India was undoubtedly Gandhi's regret in the realm of politics, the creation of a tolerant, independent India was his chief accomplishment. After partition, sectarian violence largely came to an end in India. While there is occasional violence between Hindus and Muslims, by and large there is peace. Today, Muslims

REMEMBERING GANDHI

Today Gandhi is remembered in films, commemorated with statues, and discussed frequently in the context of nonviolent resistance. Gandhi's most famous appearance in popular culture is without a doubt the movie *Gandhi*, released in 1982. It is an epic film, stretching more than three hours, that details much of Gandhi's life. Gandhi is played by Ben Kingsley (whose long career includes the role of Trevor Slattery in *Iron Man 3*), and he won an Academy Award for his performance. The film was a massive hit around the world and shaped the way that a generation viewed Gandhi the man.

Interest in Gandhi has undergone a rather striking reawakening in recent years in India. In 2006, a comedy by the name of

Ben Kingsley portrays Gandhi in the 1982 biopic film.

Lage Raho Munna Bhai dealt with his legacy on nonviolent protest. Set in modern times, the main character takes Gandhi as an example to help people around him. He names his practice of Gandhi's ideas "*Gandhigiri*"–an invented word. Since the comedy aired, *Gandhigiri* has become a popular concept in modern India. People inspired by the idea have led nonviolent protests and other public acts in the style of Gandhi.

Outside the subcontinent, statues and places named after Gandhi are scattered around virtually the entire world, contributing to perhaps Gandhi's most visible legacy. In places as diverse as Great Britain, South Africa, and the United States, Gandhi can be seen in works of art–his unmistakable appearance and dress plain for all to see.

Statues of Gandhi have caused controversy on some occasions. In 2016, one such statue was removed from the campus of the University of Ghana. Students protested that his statue should be removed because of his early writings, which are quite racist against black South Africans. While this is a matter of fact, Gandhi supporters argue that he changed his views later in life and that his early racism should be looked at in the context of the times–racism was commonplace in the South Africa of Gandhi's day.

Jawaharlal Nehru founded a political dynasty. His daughter, Indira Gandhi (unrelated to Mahatma), was the third prime minister of India.

make up 14 percent of India's population, and sectarian violence is rare.

Gandhi's old friend and political ally Jawaharlal Nehru became the first prime minister upon independence. He remained in power for the next seventeen years, until his death in 1964. During those important early years, Nehru shaped the new nation of India into the modern state we now see. He supported a secular government that stressed Indian nationalism, rather than ethnic loyalty or a decentralized government. He also made education a priority and sought to modernize the economy, spurring industry and technological education.

Nehru was also responsible for expanding the influence of the Indian National Congress. He ensured that it stayed relevant after independence, and under his leadership it became the most powerful political party at the time. In fact, in the first fifty-two years of Indian independence, the Indian National Congress was the ruling party for all but one three-year stretch. The party of Gandhi and Nehru continues to be influential even today.

The Civil Rights Movement

Gandhi's example of Satyagraha has inspired generations around the world. His successful campaigns in South Africa and India have been taken as a model by many political leaders. In this way, his actions have doubtless prevented more violence in many places around the world. The American civil rights movement is one time frame where Gandhi's shadow looms large.

During the 1950s, segregation was the law of the land in much of America—primarily Southern states. Public facilities such as schools and libraries were segregated according to race. Blacks and whites attended different schools and could not even mingle in many private businesses. In theory, segregated schools were equal in quality, as required by the Supreme Court decision *Plessy v. Ferguson* (1896). This decision found that segregation was lawful so long as there was no disparity between services offered to blacks and whites. But in reality, segregated schools were almost always far inferior. They received less funding for staff and teaching materials, and were often housed in old, dilapidated buildings.

It was in this context that the civil rights movement began in the 1950s. Weary of segregation and discrimination, African Americans began to organize and protest against the oppressive practices of the government. With no official leader, there was much debate over the best way forward. Some leaders argued against exclusively nonviolent resistance. The most famous of these was Malcolm X. He detailed his arguments against nonviolence in a 1964 interview:

> *We don't advocate violence, but nonviolent tactics based solely on morality can only succeed when you are dealing with a basically moral people. A man who oppresses another man because of his color is not moral. It is the duty of every Afro-American to protect himself against mass murderers, bombers, lynchers, floggers, brutalizers, and exploiters. If the government is unable or unwilling to protect us, we reserve our right as citizens to defend ourselves by whatever means necessary. A man with a rifle or club can only be stopped by a person armed with a rifle or club.*

It is an argument against Gandhi's philosophy that has been made many times. Some say that Gandhi's movements succeeded only because his opponents refused to use wholesale violence against him and his supporters.

While the British killed thousands, these people say, they did not turn to mass murder.

In fact, this issue has led to one significant controversy in Gandhi's legacy. During World War II, he wrote to Hitler to urge him to seek peace and nonviolence rather than war. He also opined that resistance to Hitler should be nonviolent—even in the face of mass murder and genocide. It is a bold stance, one that many historians have not viewed favorably. To this day, scholars debate whether nonviolent resistance could have worked against the Nazis—and Gandhi continues to draw criticism for his view.

Martin Luther King Jr. was a preacher and civil rights leader.

Martin Luther King Jr.

In the end, Malcolm X's view that African Americans must defend themselves with violence did not win out. It was a charismatic preacher named Martin Luther King Jr. who rose to prominence in the civil rights movement. Although the movement never had an official leader, King was its most famous spokesperson, and he organized many of its highest-profile protests.

King was a staunch advocate of nonviolent resistance and abhorred the use of violence. Throughout his life, he turned to Gandhi for inspiration, and he utilized many of the same methods as Gandhi to fight injustice in the United States. In fact, he was so influenced by Gandhi that he went on a five-week tour of India in the middle of his work as a civil rights leader. King later wrote about his time there—praising Gandhi and arguing persuasively for nonviolent resistance:

> "
>
> *It was wonderful to be in Gandhi's land, to talk with his son, his grandsons, his cousin and other relatives; to share the reminiscences of his close comrades; to visit his ashrama, to see the countless memorials for him and finally to lay a wreath on his entombed ashes at Rajghat. I left India more convinced than ever before that nonviolent resistance is the most potent weapon available to oppressed people in their struggle for freedom. It was a marvelous thing to see the amazing results of a nonviolent campaign. The aftermath of hatred and bitterness that usually follows a violent campaign was found nowhere in India. Today a mutual friendship based on complete equality exists between the Indian and British people within the commonwealth. The way of*

acquiescence leads to moral and spiritual suicide. The way of violence leads to bitterness in the survivors and brutality in the destroyers. But, the way of nonviolence leads to redemption and the creation of the beloved community.

King became the most recognized leader of the civil rights movement in 1955 when he led the Montgomery bus boycott. At the time, whites and blacks had separate seating areas on public buses in Montgomery, Alabama. The protest started when Rosa Parks refused to give her seat to a white passenger who boarded the bus. She was arrested, and African Americans around the city began a boycott. They went through extraordinary hardship—often walking long distances to their jobs—to protest the racial segregation of the times.

King became the public face of the protest, appearing on television and denouncing the racist laws of the time. When King's opponents turned to violence, firebombing his house and black churches, King preached nonviolence and restraint. He urged his supporters to "meet hate with love" and not to respond violently. In the end, the bus boycott ended when a court found the law that allowed segregation on buses unconstitutional. It was King's first major victory.

Years later, King led one of his most famous protests in the city of Birmingham, Alabama. At the time, Birmingham was one of the most discriminatory cities in the country. The police were notorious for using violence indiscriminately against African Americans. For a month, King led boycotts, sit-ins, and marches, sometimes from a jail cell. The Birmingham police responded with arrests until their jail overflowed, and they brutally attacked protesters. Police dogs were set on peaceful marchers—including children—and high-powered fire hoses were turned on them.

The photographs of the violence sent shockwaves across the nation. It was a scene that anyone present at the Dharasana saltworks protest would have recognized—peaceful protesters marching forward to be met with violence. The result was the same as in India: the supporters of segregation were vilified around the world, and King's movement gained strength.

In 1964, King was awarded the Nobel Peace Prize for his leadership. By 1968, the civil rights movement had come to an end. A number of laws and a constitutional amendment had been passed since its start that sought to protect the rights of African Americans. States were no longer allowed to disenfranchise them or exclude them from certain neighborhoods. Discrimination in hiring and segregation in public facilities were also banned.

King turned his attention to the Vietnam War at this point. He used his high profile to argue for an end to the war. It was a controversial position at the time, and King received a great deal of criticism from both African

Americans and whites of both political parties. Many believed he was betraying the war effort and weakening the cause of greater rights for African Americans. But King was unapologetic. He was an ardent supporter of peace, and this view extended to the Vietnam War.

On April 4, 1968, King was assassinated at the age of thirty-nine. However, his message could not be silenced. He is still held up as an exemplar of nonviolence and a fierce advocate for social justice.

Apartheid in South Africa

When Gandhi departed from South Africa in 1914, the fight for equality and justice was far from over. He had won a reprieve for the persecuted Indians of the country, but not for the black majority who were poorly treated by the state. In the coming years, the treatment of blacks and Indians would continue to worsen. The white minority held political power in the country and used it to marginalize other ethnic groups.

The situation reached a boiling point in 1948. The National Party won an election advocating for apartheid—strict segregation along racial lines. They kept their campaign promise, and soon identity cards in the country were issued that included a person's race. A person's rights were determined by the race recorded on his or her card: white, Asian, coloured (of mixed heritage), or black.

The country was split into different areas that determined where people could live. Affluent areas were reserved for whites, while poor areas housed the rest of the population. This split families apart, as parents and children could be assigned different race categorizations and then be unable to even live in the same area. Furthermore, it meant that millions of black farmers around the country were forced from their land because it was now designated as only able to be owned by whites.

Eventually, blacks were restricted to owning land in "homelands," ten tiny pockets of land in South Africa that were not suited for farming or development. As a consequence, most blacks were forced to leave their homeland and live in so-called townships on the outskirts of white cities. Here, they had few rights and could not even own their house or land. Laborers could not even bring their families to these townships—they were forced to live and work in squalid conditions to support the families they left behind.

The South African government even declared the homelands to be independent from the country near the end of apartheid. This meant they could deny blacks any rights that citizenship would entail. However, the overcrowded homelands were entirely surrounded by South Africa, so they were independent in name only. In reality, they were completely dependent on the South African government for their very existence.

Everyone who was not white was eventually disenfranchised under apartheid. Additionally, education was segregated, and services offered to nonwhite pupils were far inferior. The same was true for hospitals, and satisfactory medical care was difficult to find unless you were white. In some ways, apartheid was similar to the segregation that existed in the United States during the 1950s. However, it was more extreme in other ways. Over the coming decades, apartheid was also strengthened and institutionalized to a greater degree, as segregation was being rolled back in the United States.

Nelson Mandela

One organization that sought to protect the rights of black South Africans was the African National Congress (ANC). Founded in 1912, it would play an important role in the later fight against apartheid.

The man who would come to lead this fight was Nelson Mandela. He was born in 1918 and joined the ANC in 1944 while attending law school. He quickly rose to prominence in the organization. He helped found its youth wing and soon led the Transvaal branch of the ANC. At this time, he was committed to nonviolent protest. Unlike Gandhi, he did not believe that nonviolent resistance was required due to his personal ethics. Rather, he believed it was the most practical way forward. It offered the

Nelson Mandela addresses a crowd in 1990.

chance to oppose unjust laws but also made reconciliation with whites in the future a realistic scenario—unlike guerrilla warfare.

However, in 1960, Mandela's views on nonviolence changed. On March 21, a peaceful crowd of protesters gathered to voice their opposition to South Africa's pass laws, laws that limited the ability of blacks to move around the country freely. The police panicked in the face of the crowd and opened fire, killing sixty-nine people and wounding many more. The incident shocked the international community, and Mandela abandoned his support for nonviolent resistance.

Mandela helped found an armed group that used violence to fight apartheid. Under his leadership, it sabotaged various targets such as power plants. However, it avoided killing anyone. In 1962, Mandela was arrested for his part in the sabotage and sentenced to life imprisonment. In his absence, the group he helped create turned more violent. It began bombing targets like military bases, shopping malls, and police stations that were occupied—killing dozens and wounding many more.

Mandela spent the next twenty-seven years of his life in prison. However, he remained active in the ANC and was a respected leader of the group. Over the years, he was offered his freedom many times if he would make concessions to the apartheid government. He refused. It was only in 1990 that President F. W. de Klerk released him as he set about ending apartheid. The country had finally bowed to international and domestic pressure to end the racist system.

Mandela became the first president of post-apartheid South Africa. He ensured that racial discrimination came to an end and that the white minority was not treated harshly. He set up the Truth and Reconciliation Commission, which tried to heal the divide between white and black South Africans after decades of human rights abuses and conflict. Perpetrators of violence under the apartheid system were offered amnesty for their testimony.

In 1993, Mandela and de Klerk were awarded the Nobel Peace Prize for bringing about the end of apartheid. It was an accomplishment made possible partly by the pioneering work of Gandhi in South Africa years earlier. His nonviolence inspired Mandela to follow in his footsteps for most of his political career. Mandela himself acknowledged the debt that South Africa had toward Gandhi in a speech delivered in 1993:

> “
>
> *Mahatma Gandhi came to this country one hundred years ago, to assist Indians brought to this country as indentured laborers and those who came to set up trading posts. He came here to assist them to retain their right to be on a common voters roll. The Mahatma is an integral part of our history because it is here that he first experimented with truth; here that he demonstrated his characteristic firmness in pursuit of justice; here that he developed Satyagraha as a philosophy and a method of struggle …*
>
> *Gandhi is most revered for his commitment to nonviolence and the Congress Movement was strongly influenced by this Gandhian philosophy, it was a philosophy that achieved the mobilization of millions of South Africans during the 1952 defiance campaign, which established the ANC as a mass based organization. The ANC and its congress alliance partners worked jointly to protest the pass laws and the racist ideologies of the white political parties.*

Between Gandhi's departure from South Africa and the end of apartheid in South Africa, nearly eighty years had elapsed. But in the end, Gandhi's philosophy of nonviolence and truth brought about the end to the injustice of apartheid in the country he lived in for twenty-one years.

Father of the Nation

Gandhi was not the first to advocate nonviolent resistance, but he cemented its reputation as a powerful tool to fight injustice. His successful campaigns in South Africa and India inspired many to follow in his footsteps. These campaigns were the first time nonviolence was used on a grand scale to effect huge political changes. His own devotion to his cause and willingness to sacrifice in pursuit of truth and justice led to his reputation as a saint. Since his death, his reputation has only grown as figures like Mandela, King, and Barack Obama have pointed to his actions as inspiration for their own.

The methods he employed in his Satyagrahas continue to be used around the world by those fighting injustice. It is to these methods that the civil rights leaders of the future will look as they fight for change and peace. Gandhi's movements proved definitively that the voices of the people can be heard without bloodshed. It is a legacy worth celebrating.

CHRONOLOGY

1869 Gandhi is born in the Indian state of Gujarat.

1885 The Indian National Congress is founded.

1891 Gandhi passes the bar and returns to India from England.

1893 Gandhi arrives in South Africa and experiences firsthand the rampant discrimination of the times.

1894 The Natal Indian Congress is founded by Gandhi to fight injustices in South Africa.

1906 The Black Act is passed in South Africa, and Gandhi calls for resistance.

1914 The Indian Relief Act is passed in South Africa, ending some injustices there, and Gandhi departs the country.

1919 The Amritsar Massacre occurs, eroding support for British rule in India.

1920 Gandhi launches his first major Satyagraha in India: the noncooperation movement.

1930 Gandhi leads the Salt March Satyagraha and illegally collects salt from the sea.

1942 The Quit India campaign is launched by Gandhi and the leadership of the Indian National Congress.

1947 India achieves independence from Great Britain and is partitioned into the states of India and Pakistan.

1948 A Hindu extremist assassinates Gandhi.

GLOSSARY

ahimsa Nonviolence; an important concept in many Indian religions that Gandhi applied to the political sphere.

ashram A Sanskrit word for a spiritual center or monastery.

bapu The Hindi word for "father"; it is often used as a nickname for Gandhi.

caste A social class among Hindus in India. Castes were hereditary, and historically, untouchables were discriminated against. Today, castes are losing their importance in India, and discrimination is criminalized.

disenfranchise To take away someone's right to vote.

Gujarati The local language of Gujarat. It has more than fifty million speakers.

hegemony Rule or authority.

Indian subcontinent A geographic region that usually includes the modern-day countries of India, Pakistan, and Bangladesh (which was part of Pakistan upon partition), as well as Bhutan, Maldives, Nepal, and Sri Lanka.

lathi A long wooden baton, often tipped with metal, used to disperse crowds.

lingua franca A common language used by people who do not share the same first language.

Mahatma A Sanskrit word meaning "Great Soul"; it is used as another name for Gandhi on account of his accomplishments.

Mussalmans An archaic word that has been replaced by "Muslims."

neophyte A convert; someone who has just adopted a belief.

plaintiff A person who brings a lawsuit to court.

proxy war A war fought indirectly by major powers through influencing the nations that are fighting.

redress Compensation for an injury.

Sanskrit An important language throughout Indian history. Today, it has no native speakers, but many educated Indians still learn it, and sacred Hindu texts are written in it.

Satyagraha A Sanskrit word that means "truth-force"; it was the name Gandhi gave to his style of nonviolent protest.

swaraj From the Hindi word for "self-rule," swaraj was the aim and rallying cry of those seeking Indian independence from Great Britain.

untouchables Members of the lowest caste; untouchables were often discriminated against and forced to live in extreme poverty due to their status.

viceroy The rulers of the British Raj; they represented the British monarch in India.

FURTHER INFORMATION

Books

Gandhi, Mohandas K. *Autobiography: The Story of My Experiments with Truth*. Mineola, NY: Dover Publications, 1983.

Holmes, Anthony. *South Africa: History in an Hour*. New York: HarperCollins Publishers, 2012.

Ivanov, Alex. *Gandhi*. Boston: New Word City, 2016.

Walsh, Judith E. *A Brief History of India*. 2nd ed. New York: Facts on File, 2011.

Websites

Gandhi: Reckless Teenager to Father of India

http://www.bbc.co.uk/timelines/zpdqmp3

The BBC presents a timeline of Gandhi's life.

Mahatma Gandhi

https://www.sscnet.ucla.edu/southasia/History/Gandhi/gandhi.html

This comprehensive site authored by a UCLA professor includes a section about the history and politics of India.

Videos

"Mahatma Gandhi: An Unpeaceful End"

http://www.biography.com/video/mahatma-gandhi-an-unpeaceful-end-2179183345

The Biography Channel presents a short video about Gandhi and the assassination that ended his life.

"Nelson Mandela: Champion of Freedom"

http://www.history.com/topics/nelson-mandela/videos/nelson-mandela-champion-of-freedom

The History Channel spotlights the life and work of Nelson Mandela.

BIBLIOGRAPHY

Bandyopadhyay, Sekhar. *From Plassey to Partition: A History of Modern India*. Telangana, India: Orient Blackswan, 2004.

Chandra, Bipan. *India's Struggle for Independence*. London, UK: Penguin, 1989.

Dalrymple, William. "The East India Company: The Original Corporate Raider." *Guardian*, March 4, 2015. https://www.theguardian.com/world/2015/mar/04/east-india-company-original-corporate-raiders.

David, Saul. *The India Mutiny: 1857*. London, UK: Penguin, 2003.

Desai, Ashwin, and Goolam Vahed. *The South African Gandhi: Stretcher-Bearer of Empire*. Palo Alto, CA: Stanford University Press, 2015.

Gandhi, Mahatma. *Satyagraha in South Africa*, Translated from the Gujarati by Valji Govindji Desai. Ahmedabad, India: Navajivan Publishing House, 1961.

Hardiman, David. "Towards a History of Non-violent Resistance." *Economic and Political Weekly* 48, no. 23 (June 8, 2013): 41–48.

Homer, Jack A., ed. *The Gandhi Reader: A Sourcebook of His Life and Writings*. New York: Grove Press, 1994.

Huttenback, Robert. *Gandhi in South Africa: British Imperialism and the Indian Question, 1860– 1914*. Ithaca, NY: Cornell University Press, 1971.

Lloyd, Nick. "Amritsar Massacre: How Britain Lost the Will to Rule." *Telegraph*, January 3, 2014. http://www.telegraph.co.uk/history/world-war-one/inside-first-world-war/part-five/10544286/amritsar-massacre.html.

MacFarlane, Charles, and Thomas Thomson. *The Comprehensive History of England: Civil and Military, Religious, Intellectual, and Social, from the Earliest Period to the Suppression of the Sepoy Revolt*. London, UK: Blackie and Son, 1859.

Namier, Sir Lewis, and John Brooke. *The History of Parliament: The House of Commons 1754–1790*. London, UK: Oxford University Press for the History of Parliament Trust, 1864.

Nanda, B. R. *Mahatma Gandhi: A Biography*. London, UK: Oxford University Press, 1996.

Sen, S. N. *History of the Freedom Movement in India (1857–1947)*. New Delhi, India: New Age International, 1997.

Strangman, Thomas Joseph. *Indian Courts and Characters*. London, UK: W. Heinemann, 1931.

INDEX

Page numbers in **boldface** are illustrations. Entries in **boldface** are glossary terms.

ABOUT THE AUTHOR

Derek Miller is a writer and educator from Salisbury, Maryland. His books include *Health in Contemporary Africa*, *The Economy in Contemporary Africa*, and *Henry David Thoreau: Civil Disobedience*, among many others. When Derek is not writing or researching, he enjoys traveling with his wife.